THE GROWING BODY

All bodies grow. Humans begin life as a BABY. A baby has a large head compared with its body, arms and legs.

A TODDLER is much larger than a baby, but is a similar shape. The lower part of the body — called the tummy or belly — sticks out.

baby   toddler

When a child reaches the age of three, **muscles** form that hold the tummy in. The body, arms and legs grow longer, but the head *still seems* large.

By the age of four, the head is nearly the *size* of an adult's head. The rest of the body *will* keep growing for about another fourteen years.

four year old

eighteen year old

5

SKIN

The human body is covered in SKIN. An adult's skin is about the size of a tablecloth that is roughly 2 metres long and 2 metres wide.

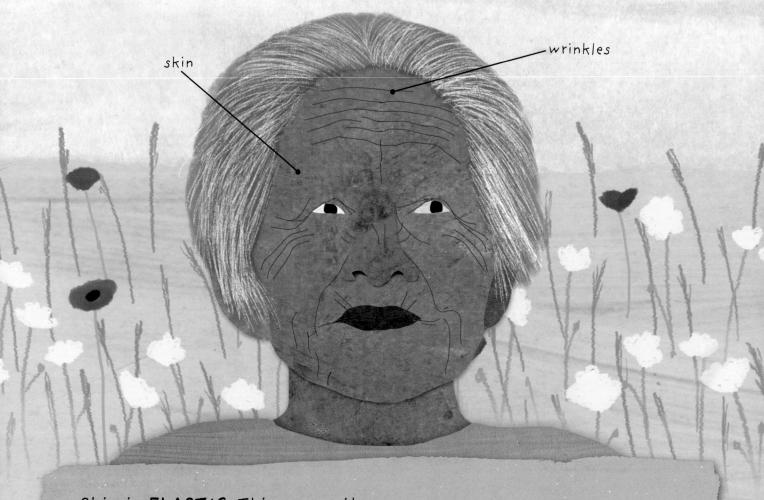

skin

wrinkles

Skin is **ELASTIC.** This means it can s-t-r-e-t-c-h. If you pinch the skin on the back of your hand you stretch it. Let it go and the skin springs back.

Skin becomes less elastic as you get older. If an older person pinches the skin on the back of their hand, it takes a few seconds for the skin to go back down.

Can you tell which hand belongs to an older person?

W
FRANKLIN WATTS

Franklin Watts
Published in paperback in Great Britain in 2019 by The Watts Publishing Group

Credits
Series Editor: Amy Stephenson
Series Designer: Krina Patel
Illustrations: Krina Patel
Picture Researcher: Amy Stephenson / Diana Morris

Picture Credits: Tudor Antone Adrian/Dreamstime: 21c. AFPics/Shutterstock: 11c. Algarabi/Dreamstime: front cover bca, 23b, 28bl. Ilya Andriianou/Shutterstock: 25c. Ilya Andriyanov/Shutterstock: 27ca. Marilyn Barbone/Dreamstime: 9t. Bentaboe/Dreamstime: front cover br, 19b, 29bc. Blend Images/Shutterstock: 27cr. Blickwinkel/Alamy: 16t. Maksym Bondarchuk/Shutterstock: 12t. Kelly Boreson/Shutterstock: 18bc. ChalyonSOZI/Shutterstock: 6b. Jean Paul Chassenet/Dreamstime: 16b. comodigit/Shutterstock: 11t. Gary Cooper/Dreamstime: 9b. cvadrat/Dreamstime: 21b. Peter Dazeley/Getty Images: 26r. devil79sd/Shutterstock: 16c. Dgrilla/Dreamstime: 14t. espies/Shutterstock: 21t. Fleckstone/Shutterstock: 13t. J M Gelpi/Shutterstock: 5tr. Stephen Gibson/Dreamstime: 17t. David Gilder/Dreamstime: 5b. Antonio Guillem/Shutterstock: 18c. imagebroker/Alamy: 22b. itsjustme/Shutterstock: 23cl, 23cr, 24tr. Juefraphoto/Shutterstock: 10t. Sebastian Kaulitzki/Shutterstock: 27b. Keechman/Dreamstime: 17c. Konstantin Kolidzei/Dreamstime: 8t, 28bla. D. Kucharski K. Kucharska/Shutterstock: 11b, 28bca. La64/Dreamstime: 19t. luxxtek/Getty Images: back cover t, 26tl. mimagephotography/Shutterstock: 17b. Morrowlight/Dreamstime: 5c. Oleksil Natykach/Shutterstock: 27t. Tyler Olson/Shutterstock: 20t. Kirsty Pargeter/Dreamstime: 4t. Tatiana Popova/Shutterstock: 18t. Rocketclips, Inc/Shutterstock: 20c. Jesada Sabai/Shutterstock: 23t. Sabphoto/Shutterstock: 25t. schanke/Shutterstock: front cover bl, 22t, 29bca. Science Photo Library: back cover cl, 19cl. Science Pics/Dreamstime: 25b. Pavel Shiykov/Shutterstock: 14c. Nathalie Speliers/Dreamstime: 18br. Spirokwok/Dreamstime: 15c. Stochaz/Dreamstime: 7b. Stockphotosart/Shutterstock: 15b, 29bla. Suravid/Shutterstock: 5tl. Vincius Tupinamba/Dreamstime: front cover bc, 19c, 29bl. Warrengoldswain/Dreamstime: 7t. Pan Xunbin/Shutterstock: 13b. Ziviani/Shutterstock: back cover cr, 27cl, 28bc. Chad Zuber/Shutterstock: 24tl. Zurijeta/Shutterstock: 7c.

ISBN: 978 1 4451 4648 5

Printed in China

Franklin Watts
An imprint of
Hachette Children's Group
Part of The Watts Publishing Group
Carmelite House
50 Victoria Embankment
London EC4Y 0DZ

An Hachette UK Company
www.hachette.co.uk

www.franklinwatts.co.uk

To Gordon and family – PR

To Sam, Dhilan, Leila, Lilly and Oscar – KP

CONTENTS

⚠ This symbol shows where there is some advice
or some information to help you stay safe.
Words in **bold** can be found in the glossary on page 30.

THE HUMAN BODY

Everyone has a body. The human body has many parts. In this book you will look at parts on the outside and parts on the inside of the body.

You can find out many curious things about the human body in this book. Sometimes you have to guess what you see, then turn the page to find the answer.

Near the end of this book is our human body curiosity box. You can talk about it with your friends. You can make your own curiosity box about the human body.

4

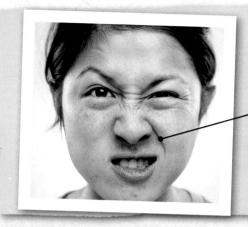

You can see how elastic skin is when you pull funny faces. Your skin forms patterns of RIDGES for one funny face. They disappear and change to another pattern of ridges when you pull another funny face.

As we get older, the skin of the face forms ridges that do not disappear. They are called WRINKLES.

WHAT CAN THIS BE?

A pattern of ridges on a face?

A pattern of ridges on a foot?

A pattern of ridges on a fingertip?
Turn the page to find out.

It's a pattern of ridges on a fingertip!

If you dip your fingertip lightly in ink, paint or butter and press it onto a smooth surface, you will be able to see a pattern of ridges. This is called a FINGERPRINT.

There are three main types of fingerprint.

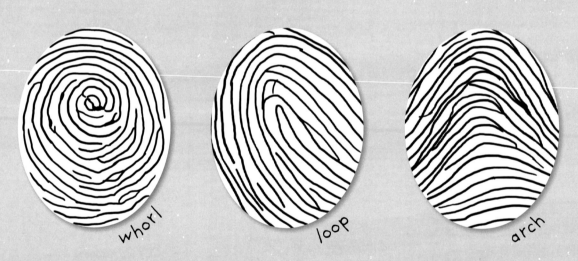

whorl   loop   arch

You may have different patterns on different fingers.
Fingerprints stay the same all your life.
Nobody else has fingerprints like yours.
They are special to you.

FRECKLES AND SKIN COLOUR

Freckles are brown patches of skin where the skin has made large amounts of a substance called melanin (mel-ah-nin).

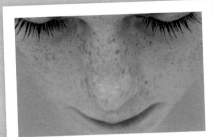

This girl has lots of freckles all over her nose and cheeks.

Melanin is found in all skin. It helps to give the skin its colour, which can range from dark to light.

DAMAGED SKIN

Skin can easily be damaged. Sometimes the damage comes from outside the body. Other times the damage comes from inside the body.

The Sun sends out **rays** of light that we can see. It also sends out rays of **ultraviolet** light that we can't see. These rays can burn the skin. This is called SUNBURN and it can be dangerous.

⚠ Never look directly at the Sun. Its light can damage your eyes!

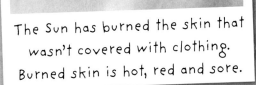

The Sun has burned the skin that wasn't covered with clothing. Burned skin is hot, red and sore.

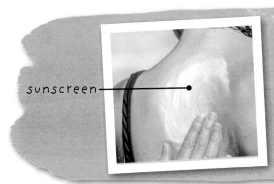
sunscreen

The best way to PROTECT the skin from sunburn is to put sunscreen on the skin, wear a hat with a wide brim and stay in the shade on sunny days.

When skin is rubbed hard, burned or frozen, a BLISTER can form. Clear liquid, called **plasma**, flows under the damaged skin and forms a bubble.

New skin grows, and in time the bubble pops and the damaged skin above it falls away.

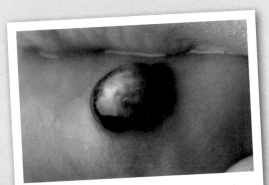
Sometimes blood is the liquid in the bubble. This is called a blood blister.

WHAT CAN THIS BE?

A scab?
A wart?
A blister?
Turn the page to find out.

It's a wart!

Warts are made when a certain kind of **virus** (vy-rus) enters the skin.

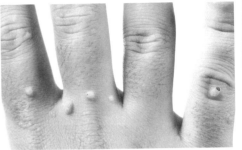

One wart may grow or there may be a group of warts. Warts can last on the skin for some time.

In time, the warts on this person's fingers will probably disappear.

When a wart forms on the sole of the foot it is called a VERRUCA. Sometimes a few can grow at once. They will usually vanish in time, like warts.

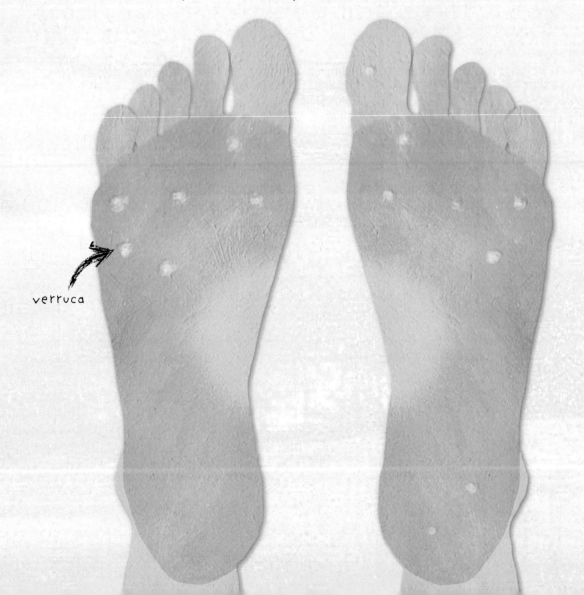

verruca

BLOOD flows inside your body in tiny tubes called blood vessels. If you bang your skin, the blood vessels may break and blood flows out under the skin.

The blood stays there for some time and makes a coloured patch called a BRUISE.

A bruise can be many colours, such as black, red or purple, and even green and yellow.

skin cross-section

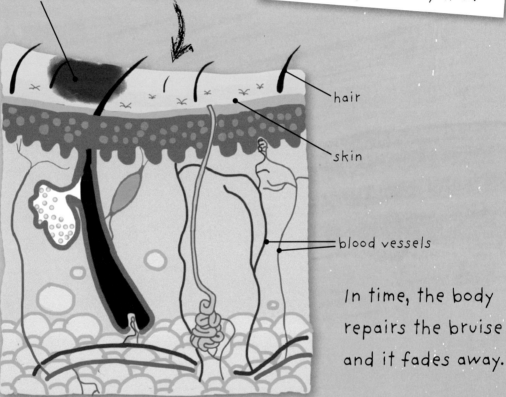

hair

skin

blood vessels

In time, the body repairs the bruise and it fades away.

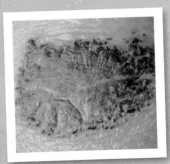

If you cut yourself, blood flows out of the WOUND. As the blood **clots** and dries, it seals up the wound.

In time, the dried blood forms a SCAB, which keeps out **germs** until new skin has been made.

NAILS AND HAIR

Hair and nails keep growing throughout our lives. People cut both their hair and their nails to stop them growing too long.

NAILS grow on the tops of the ends of fingers and toes. They protect the fingers and toes from cuts and bruises.

They are made of the same hard material as claws, hooves and horns in other animals. This material is called keratin (keh-rah-tin), and it is made of dead skin **cells**.

human nails

cat claws

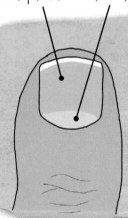

nail plate . lanula

There are TWO PARTS to the nail that we can see. The small moon or lanula (lan-yoo-lah) and the nail plate, which sits on top of the nail bed.

Nails grow s...l...o...w...l...y, at about 3 mm a month.

14

Hair grows faster than nails, it grows at about 12 mm a month.
There are about one hundred thousand HAIRS on a human head. Hairs
can be black, brown, blonde or red. Hair can be curly, wavy or straight.

blonde and wavy

black and curly

red and straight

If you look at your arm, you can see hairs sticking out of your skin. Hair grows all over your body, except on the palms of your hands, the soles of your feet, and your lips.

Every hair grows out of a hole in your skin. Some hairs can be very short, thin and hard to see.

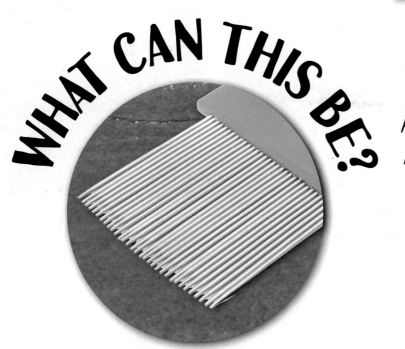

WHAT CAN THIS BE?

A musical instrument?
An ordinary comb?
A nit comb?
Turn the page to find out.

NITS, SPOTS AND SWEAT

It's a nit comb!

It is used to take nits out of the hair.

A nit is the EGG
of the head louse.

HEAD LICE are tiny **insects**
that can live on human hair.

When a head louse wants a meal, it bites
into the skin on the scalp and drinks the
blood. This makes your head itchy.

A nit comb removes the eggs and washing
with special shampoo removes the head lice.

As hair grows out of its hole, it gets covered in OIL called sebum (see-bum), which is made by your body. Sebum makes skin **waterproof**. If sebum mixes with flakes of skin and blocks the hole, it makes a SPOT.

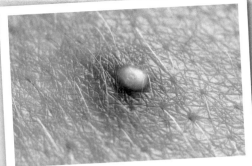

If a spot gets **infected**, a white substance called **pus** forms inside the spot!

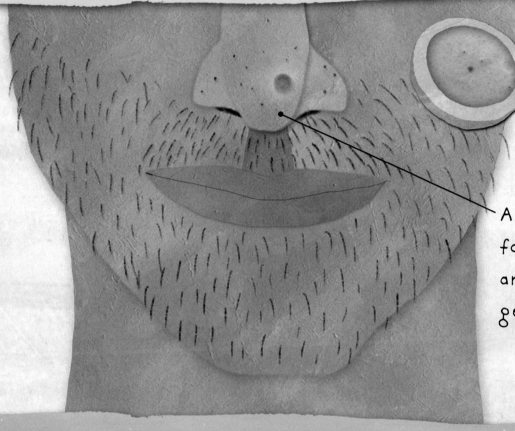

A BLACKHEAD forms if the oil and skin flakes get dirt in them.

There are other holes in the skin called PORES. A liquid called SWEAT is made in them when you get hot. Sweat flows out of your pores and cools the skin.

If sweat stays on your skin for a while it can make you smell.

This man has lots of beads of sweat all over his face because he is hot.

SENSES

Humans have five senses. Our senses work together to tell us about the world.

The SKIN is sensitive to TOUCH. It can tell you if something is smooth, rough, sharp, hot or cold.

An apple feels smooth and cool if you hold it in your hand.

People like to smell things that smell good, such as a flower!

The NOSE is sensitive to SMELLS in the air. The part that **detects** smells is high up inside the nose, so you have to sniff to smell something.

The TONGUE is used to TASTE food and drink. There are five tastes the **taste buds** on the tongue can detect: salt, savoury, sour, sweet and bitter.

a sweet-tasting lollipop

close-up of the tongue's surface

18

The EARS are sensitive to SOUNDS. They let us hear them. Sounds travel through the air as waves that we cannot see. The outside of the ear collects the waves and sends them into the earhole where the sounds can be heard.

People can collect more sound by cupping their hands around their ears.

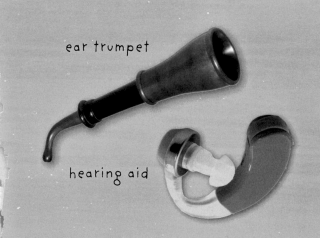

ear trumpet

hearing aid

Some people are DEAF. This means they can't hear well or sometimes at all. In the past, people used an ear trumpet to help them hear.

Today, hearing aids are used to help people hear.

WHAT CAN THIS BE?

Something for testing eyes?
Something for testing ears?
A mask?
Turn the page to find out.

It's something for testing eyes!

An **optician** uses a trial frame to find out how well a person can see.

Eyes are sensitive to light. They give us the sense of SIGHT. They have many parts that help us see. One part inside each eye is called the LENS.

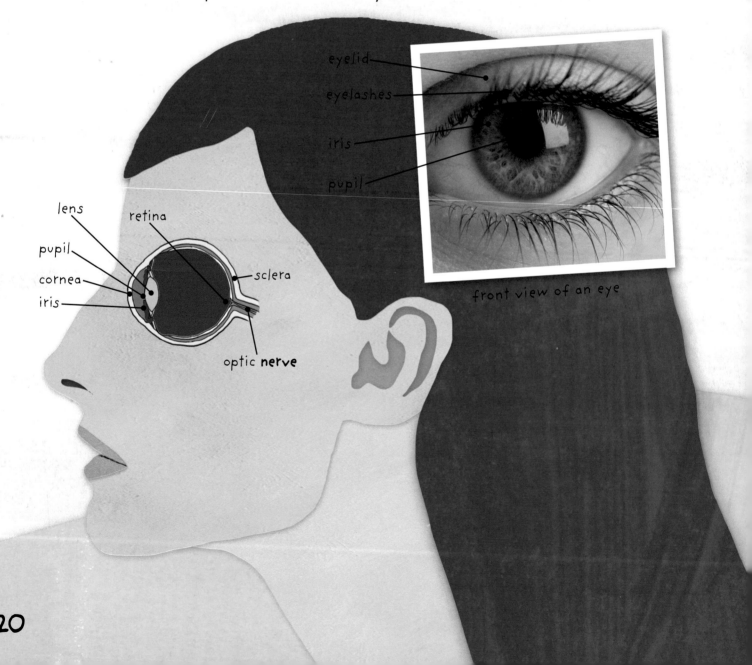

eyelid

eyelashes

iris

pupil

lens

retina

pupil

cornea

iris

sclera

optic **nerve**

front view of an eye

20

If a lens doesn't work properly you cannot see clearly out of that eye. Things that are either far away or close by may look **blurry**.

If you cannot see well an optician may tell you that you need to wear GLASSES.

The lenses in a pair of glasses do the same job as the lenses in your eyes.

Even when you can see clearly, some things can fool your eyes.

Which of the pink circles is the largest?

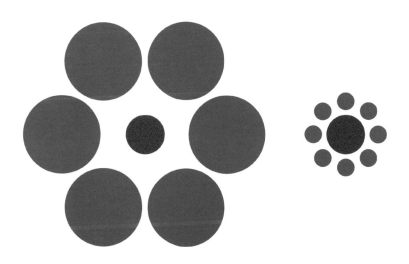

What can you see between the grey squares?

The pink circles are both the same size and you should see grey patches in the cross-shaped spaces between the grey squares. These are both optical illusions - something that tricks your eyes into seeing something.

21

TEETH AND BONES

Teeth and bones are hard parts of our bodies.
Bones give our bodies shape and teeth help us eat food.

There are two parts to every TOOTH. The part you can see above the gums is called the crown. The part inside the gums is called the root.

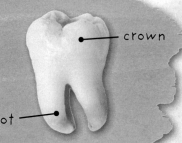

crown

root

There are three types of tooth in your mouth.

The canines (cay-nines) are a pointed shape. They are used to tear food.

The molars (moh-lars) are a cube shape. They are used to chew food

The INCISORS (in-sy-zores) are a square shape. They are used to cut through food.

decay

gum

People have two sets of teeth. The first teeth are called the MILK TEETH. The second teeth are called the permanent teeth.

At about six years old, a child's milk teeth lose their roots. This makes each tooth wobble and fall out. A permanent tooth grows in its place.

⚠️ You must look after your teeth. Brushing them with toothpaste every day will help stop tooth decay.

If you squeeze your finger you will feel something hard under the skin. It is a FINGER BONE.

Each finger has three bones in it. Each thumb has two bones in it.

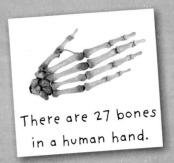

There are 27 bones in a human hand.

You can feel bones in other parts of the body.

Rub your fingers down your chest to feel your ribs.

Rub a thumb down the middle of your back and feel the lumps of your backbone or spine.

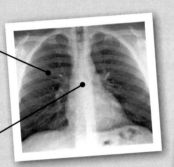

Feel for a bone at your elbow.

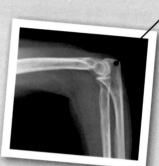

WHAT CAN THIS BE?

An X-ray of an elbow?
An X-ray of a knee?
An X-ray of a foot?

Turn the page to find out.

23

SKELETON AND MUSCLES
It's an X-ray of a knee!

Doctors use **X-ray** machines to take photographs of the inside of a body.

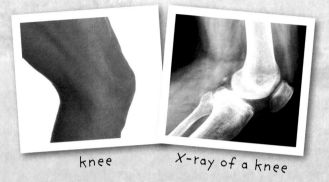

knee   X-ray of a knee

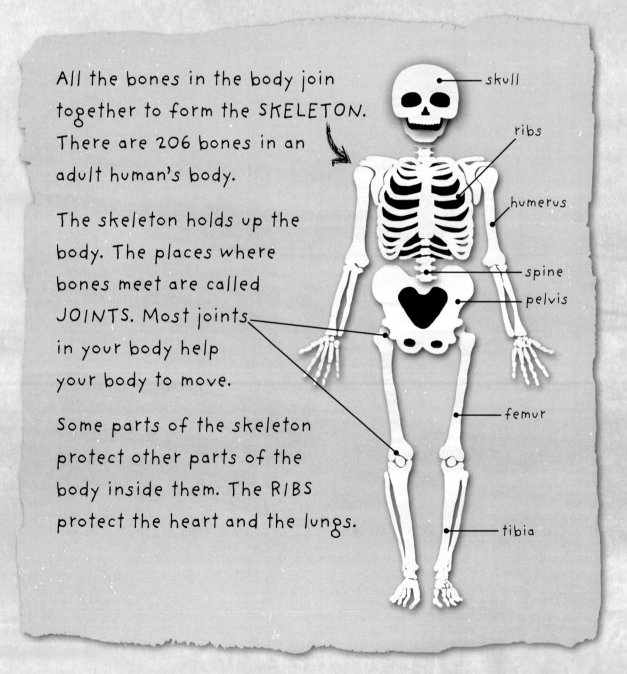

All the bones in the body join together to form the SKELETON. There are 206 bones in an adult human's body.

The skeleton holds up the body. The places where bones meet are called JOINTS. Most joints in your body help your body to move.

Some parts of the skeleton protect other parts of the body inside them. The RIBS protect the heart and the lungs.

skull

ribs

humerus

spine

pelvis

femur

tibia

Bones cannot move on their own. They need MUSCLES to move them. Muscles are softer than bones but they can become a bit harder when they work.

The muscles in the upper arm are called BICEPS. Biceps are soft when the arm is straight.

When the biceps work, they pull up the bones in the lower arm. Working biceps will feel harder than biceps that are not working. You can see the muscles move under the skin.

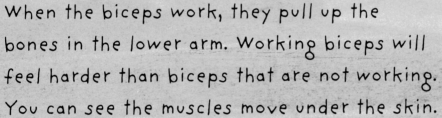

Bones, muscles and **ligaments** found in the legs

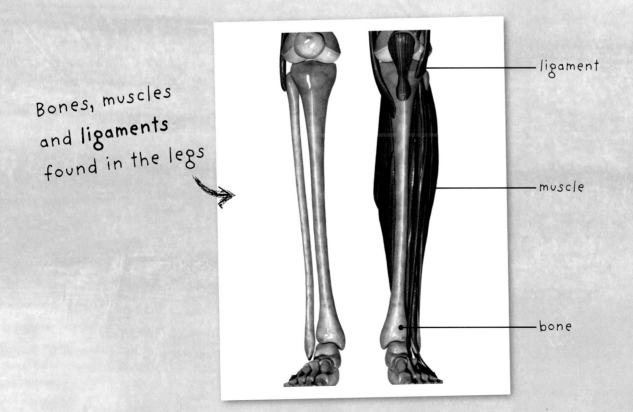

ligament

muscle

bone

INSIDE THE BODY

You cannot see most of what is inside your body. Underneath your skin, your organs are hard at work.

These models are of the organs inside the body. The main organs are the brain, heart, lungs, stomach, small intestine, large intestine and liver.

They all have different jobs to do.

brain: thinking; controlling the body

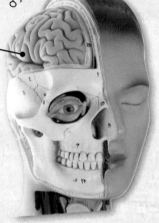

lungs: breathing

heart: pumping blood

liver: storing food, cleaning your blood; helping **digestion**

stomach: digesting food

large intestine: **absorbing** water; transporting waste

small intestine: absorbing digested food into the blood

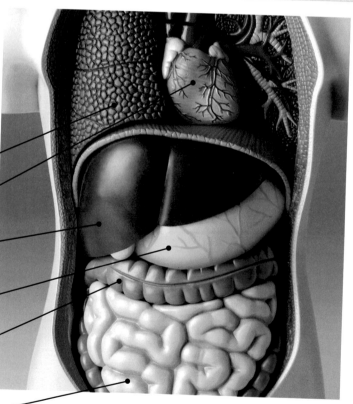

All the parts of the body work together to keep you alive!

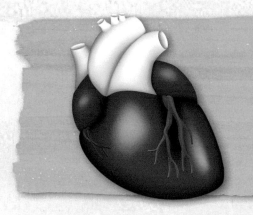

The heart pumps the blood around the body. It makes a sound called a HEARTBEAT as it works. A heartbeat sounds like 'lub dup'.

Your heart is in your chest, but you can feel its beat at your wrist as a PULSE. Press two fingers against your wrist to feel your pulse.

A doctor uses a **stethoscope** to listen to sounds inside the body.

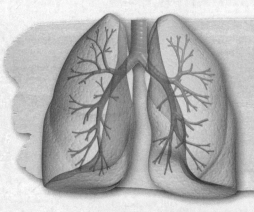

A doctor also uses a stethoscope to listen to air going in and out of the LUNGS. If the lungs are not healthy the doctor will hear wheezing and crackling sounds.

Have you ever put your ear to someone's tummy to hear the sounds it makes?

HUMAN BODY CURIOSITY BOX

A curiosity box is a place to put all of the curious things you have collected.

What items are in your human body curiosity box?

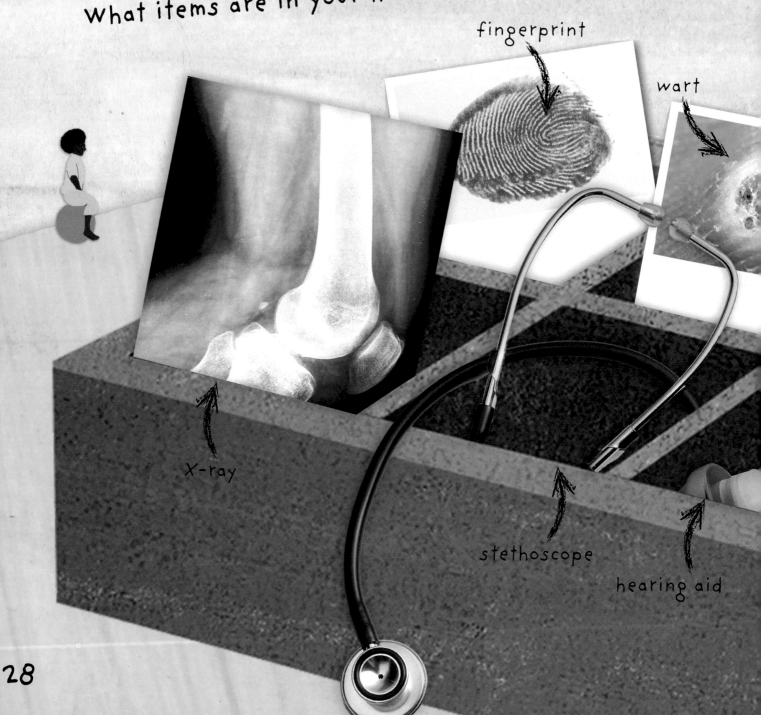

fingerprint

wart

X-ray

stethoscope

hearing aid

CURIOUS QUIZ

1. Where do you find wrinkles?
a) in the hair
b) on the teeth
c) in the skin

2. What do you get when your skin is rubbed hard?
a) a wart
b) a blister
c) a blackhead

3. Roughly how many hairs are there on a human head?
a) one thousand
b) one hundred thousand
c) one million

4. What is a head louse egg called?
a) a nit
b) a verruca
c) a scab

5. What is the black hole in the centre of the eye called?
a) the pupil
b) the iris
c) the retina

6. Where are your incisors?
a) in your ear
b) up your nose
c) in your mouth

Curious quiz answers: 1c; 2b; 3b; 4a; 5a; 6c.
The hand with the wrinkly skin on page 6 belongs to the older person.

nit comb

tooth

eyetest trial frame

GLOSSARY

absorb to take in or soak up

blurry objects with fuzzy edges; something that is hard to see in detail

cells tiny structures – often called 'building blocks' – because they make up the parts of the body

clot when fluid, such as blood, turns from a liquid to a solid, in this case a scab

detect to notice or identify something

digest to break down food so it can be used by the body

elastic a material that springs back to its original shape and size after it has been stretched

germs microscopic organisms that cause diseases

infected part of a body invaded with harmful germs

insect animals with six legs, and usually one or two pairs of wings. (The head louse doesn't have any wings)

ligament a short band of tough, bendy material that joins bones together

muscles parts of the body that can become shorter and pull on other body parts to make them move

nerves long, thin structures that carry signals to all parts of the body to make it work

optic to do with the eye

optician a person who tests people's eyes to finds out if they have any eye problems

plasma a yellow liquid that carries other parts of blood

pus a white, yellow or brown liquid made by the body as it kills harmful germs

ray light and heat that travels in a straight line

stethoscope a medical instrument used to listen to sounds inside the body

taste buds parts of the tongue that detect tastes

ultraviolet light we can't see but which carries a lot of energy that can be harmful

virus something that can reproduce in the cells of a human body and cause disease

waterproof a material that water can't pass through

X-ray a special type of photograph that shows the inside of the body

CURIOUS FACTS

CURIOUS BEGINNINGS

People have collected objects for thousands of years. During the 1500s and 1600s, special cabinets were made to display the objects that were brought back from voyages to newly-discovered lands, such as North America. These cabinets were sometimes whole rooms, which became the first museums. In time, some museums became medical museums.

WHAT IS A CURIOSITY BOX?

A curiosity box is a small copy of these cabinets. It is a more scientific way of displaying items than a nature table. You can group items together by theme. Children are naturally curious about their bodies, and as they grow up they visit doctors and dentists, and they become further aware of how their bodies work. In the past, as the study of medicine developed, museums were set up to house bodies and their parts for further study. In this book the focus is on the features of the body the children may examine as part of their everyday lives. As these features may change over time photographs could be taken and inserted in the curiosity box.

YOUR CURIOSITY BOX

It's easy to make your own curiosity box. A shoebox or other small cardboard box will do! Ask an adult to help you cut long strips of card with slits cut into them. Slot them together to make lots of small sections inside your box. Place the photographs you take inside the sections.

People sometimes keep milk teeth or a lock or hair as a memento of a life event. With care these could form part of the curiosity box collection. You may find information on preserving teeth and hair on the Internet but you should also follow advice for educational institutions such as the reference to the ASE below. Plastic models of bodies, eyes and ears could be added to a curiosity box. Young children may like to add instruments from their doctors and nurses kits too.

USEFUL INFORMATION AND WEBLINKS

For general information on practical science, contact the Association for Science Education at **www.ase.org.uk** for their book, *Be Safe!* (Fourth Edition).

Some museums — especially science museums — have sections relating to health, the body and medicine. Check the websites of those near you to see if they may be suitable for young children.

HUMAN BODY NOTES

Here is some more information, for parents and teachers, on the parts of the human body found in this book.

The human body
Early on in many primary science courses, children are introduced to the parts of the body. This usually begins by naming (and spelling) the external body parts. Children are familiar with skeletons from cartoons and scary stories, and so a look at the skeleton may also be a feature of this early part of body studies.

The life cycle of humans is also a feature of many early primary science courses and this is lightly referenced on page 5. Reference to ageing, in connection with the skin, is made on pages 6–7. You may like to begin a body curiosity box project by collecting photographs of family members when they were babies, toddlers, teenagers and adults.

Skin
You may like to let the children explore their skin with a magnifying glass and describe what they see. This may serve as an introduction to other skin features later in the book. A child may recall that they have had flaky skin, and this gives an opportunity to say that the skin is always flaking off, but in very small bits. These join with other tiny pieces of material, such as soil particles, hairs, fibres from paper and clothes, and pollen grains to form dust.

The children could test the back of hands of people of different ages and photograph any ridges that are slow to sink down for their curiosity box. They may also like to photograph their own funny faces to show the elasticity of their skin.

Fingerprints, freckles and skin colour
Children can look at their own fingerprints by examining the tips of their fingers with a magnifying glass. They could make a permanent print for their curiosity box by rolling each fingertip over an ink pad, then rolling it over white paper.

Damaged skin
The text about preventing sunburn is basic, but you may wish to discuss other strategies, such as wearing long trousers, shirts with sleeves and keeping out of the sun during the hottest part of the day – between the hours of 11 a.m. and 3 p.m.

When the opportunity arises, a photograph could be taken of a blister for the curiosity box.

Sometimes verrucas can become so hard that they are painful to walk on. A chiropodist can advise about their removal.

Children must be warned against picking scabs (this increases the risk of infection) and against keeping them for their curiosity box!

When the opportunity arises, a photograph could be taken of a wart, scab or bruise for a curiosity box. A series of photographs could be taken of a scab or bruise to show the healing process.

Nails and hair
A child can have their fingernails cut, and then the next time they are cut the clippings could be collected and photographed before they are discarded. The photograph could go in the curiosity box with a label about how long it has taken the nails to grow. This activity can be repeated with toenails.

Nits, spots and sweat
When the opportunity arises, a photograph could be taken of a pimple or a blackhead for the curiosity box.

Senses
Children aged 5–7 in the UK will study the senses as part of the national curriculum. This section can be used to support and reinforce their work.

Eyes
The illustration can be used to make a model eye out of several different colours of modelling clay. The model could go in a curiosity box.

Teeth and bones
When the opportunity arises, a photograph could be taken of a wobbly tooth in the mouth, and a photograph can be taken when it has left the mouth. A collection of tooth photographs could be made for the curiosity box as each of the milk teeth fall out.

Bones provide support for all the soft parts of the body. Some bones protect other organs of the body. For example the skull bones protect the brain and the ribs protect the heart and lungs. The joints between the bones allow parts of the body to move.

Skeleton and muscles
A child could assess the accuracy of toy skeletons or Halloween party costumes by comparing them with the skeleton illustrated on page 24.

Children can be encouraged to feel the muscles in the tops of their legs when they are sat down, then straighten their leg and feel the muscles tighten to extend the activity on page 25.

Inside the body
Children often have toy stethoscopes in doctors' and nurses' kits, so may be already be familiar with this item. Children may find it difficult to take their pulse. You could find it for them then press their fingers (not too hard) on the wrist to see if they can feel it.

Use coloured modelling clay to make a model of the organs of the body, using the illustration on page 27 to help them. The model could go in the curiosity box.